MORE FUNNY COVID MEMES

Compiled by
Ed Mickolus

More Funny Covid Memes

By Ed Mickolus

First Edition 2021

ISBN: 978-1-949173-10-9

Published in the United States by
Wandering Woods Publishers

Book Design, Cover and Typesetting by
Cynthia J. Kwitchoff (CJKCREATIVE.COM)

Also See

America's Funniest Memes: Coronavirus Edition
Complied by Ed Mickolus

INTRODUCTION

The year 2020 was rough. As I write this (mid-April 2021), more than 560,000 Americans have died, with more than three million deaths worldwide. But the memes kept on coming as well, to remind us that we are resilient, and one very public piece of evidence for this resiliency is how our sense of humor plays out.

With lockdowns around the world, audiences have not been able to attend stand-up comedy performances. But meme-writers have rushed in to fill the gap, offering up the topical observational humor formerly the realm of stand-ups. Memes offer a comedic outlet available to all. You don't have to memorize a 500-punchline hour-long set to get a laugh. You don't have to be a naturally talented speaker. You don't even have to write that much—one good one-liner is fine for meme audiences. You don't have to remember a great joke you heard—thanks to email and social media, you just hit POST, FORWARD or SEND and get credit for the shared glory of the humor. So if there's just one good thing to come out of the pandemic, it could be the ascendancy of the meme. They predated 2020 by roughly a decade, but they became our comedic currency in 2020.

I've used only unsigned/unattributed memes to avoid potential copyright infringement. I've also avoided sketch- and photo-dependent memes to keep the price of this book down for you! I've also not used the hundreds of 2020 election-specific memes—no need to irritate potential buyers of this book!

A big thank you goes to Virginia Riley, Bonnie Evans, Carol Pierskalla, Diane Tryon, Sue Jones, Greg Barry, Ruth Van Alstine, and Carol Benson, ace writers/discoverers/posters of memes, limericks, and haikus.

Ed Mickolus

TABLE OF CONTENTS

Coronavirus Diary

January 2020: This is my year! Gonna make all the things happen! May 2020: hiding under bed from global pandemic, murder hornets, the presidential election, no toilet paper, growing a Wyatt Earp mustache

January 2020: Resolves to improve my fitness, invest more, and move up in my career. December 2020: Has a favorite face mask. Gets excited finding Lysol wipes in the store. Congratulates myself for putting on pants.

Kinda feeling like the Earth just sent us all to our rooms to think about what we've done.

Anti-vaxxers currently getting a demo of a vaccine-free world.

People are making apocalypse jokes like there's no tomorrow.

Well, it's Day 272 of 15 days to flatten the curve.

If you think artists are useless, try to spend your quarantine without music, books, poems, movies, paintings, and games.

We are not all in the same boat. We are in the same storm. Some have yachts, some canoes, and some are drowning. Just be kind and help whomever you can.

This is the longest game of cooties I have ever played in my life! Where's base at? I don't wanna play no more.

Goodnight moon. Goodnight zoom. Goodnight sense of impending doom.

Due to the massive increase in deliveries, FedEx and UPS have joined forces and are now Fed-Up.

I can't believe it's almost September. Literally feels like it was March just 16 years ago.

Sometimes I wonder if all of this is happening because I didn't forward that message to 10 other people.

So I got pulled over in the HOV lane and when the cop asked where's my passenger, I told him due to social distancing he was in the car behind me.

Biggest lesson: Don't ever think it can't happen to you.

Time Person of the Year: Mayhem. Making 2020 his best year ever.

I feel like every day is the Kobayashi Maru and I am not James T. Kirk.

Welcome to the final quarter of 2020. May the odds be ever in your favor.

Because of Covid for the first time since 1945 the National Spelling Bee has been cancil... cancul... cansel... It's been called off. (Spellcheck fought me tooth and nail on this entry!)

News flash! Sticking your tongue on an outdoor bug zapper lamp will cure the virus. Yep, I read it on the Internet.

Don we now our plague apparel.

In the 1980s I was riding my bike and fell off and hurt my knee. I'm telling you this now because we didn't have social media then.

Wave 1: I'm going to make sourdough bread and learn to play piano. Wave 2: Every day that I shower and wear pants is a personal victory.

We are now officially in the fourth quarter of 2020. Man, I hope we are playing the Falcons.

We are basically all peasants again. Bake bread. Avoid plague. Revolt against tyranny.

Just slung my bra off and threw it to the other side of the couch where there are already 2 other bras. If my math is right, it's Wednesday.

I keep thinking I wouldn't mind the cooler weather to kick in but I don't want to get too enthusiastic about it because I am 100% sure this is the year we will get flammable snow.

Decades I have been alive in:

- 1980s
- 1990s
- 2000s
- 2010s
- Early 2020
- March-May 2020
- June-July 2020
- August-September 2020
- October 1, 2020
- October 2, 2020

Quarantine has given me a lot of time to slow down and reflect, which is awful.

Someone asked me if I had plans for the fall. It took me a moment to realize they meant "autumn" and not the collapse of civilization.

I've had my name mispronounced so many times that I'm not even sure if I've been saying it correctly.

People who ask me what I'm doing tomorrow probably assume I even know what day of the week it is.

"After this is all over" was a fun sentence to say back in April.

I showed my Facebook page to my psychiatrist and she wants to talk to all of you.

Spring got the South playing the game "Plague or Pollen"… good luck, y'all. #explainyoursneeze

I apologize for the coin shortage. I started a swear jar.

I'm proud to announce that I have completed the 1st item on my bucket list. I have the bucket.

I have washed my hands so much I've uncovered a night-club stamp from 25 years ago.

Chuck Norris drinks coronavirus for breakfast.

This year feels like a test that none of us studied for.

So a burglar broke into the house… I put the red dot on his chest and the cat did the rest.

I am not an early bird or a night owl. I am some form of permanently exhausted pigeon.

I'm tired of people complaining about $7 beers, $10 parking and a $20 cover charge. Don't like the prices, stop coming to my house.

What's something you started doing during quarantine but want to continue doing after it's over? Asking people to mute themselves.

At least once a day I walk outside and say, "Computer, end program", just in case.

Reminder: WalMart will be closed on Christmas Day so that both cashiers can be with their families.

Posted a photo of my clean house and it was flagged and removed as "fake news".

Since we're all going to die, if anyone is secretly in love with me, now is the time to speak up.

I asked my doctor today how long he thinks this COVID thing will last. He responded with, "How should I know? I'm a doctor, not a politician."

The air is so full of sanitizer that I'm not even getting dirty thoughts these days.

Also kind of cool that it is now polite to ring someone's door bell and then run away.

I wish Mad Magazine was still around. What a great year for satire.

At this point, I wouldn't even be surprised if the dinosaurs returned.

At this point I would feel safer if Coronavirus held a press conference telling us how it's going to save us from the Government.

Anyone else say "Shields up, Captain" when putting on a mask?

We're living in two Stephen King novels right now: The Dead Zone and The Stand. If clowns show up, I'm done. I'm just done.

I'm starting to miss the good old days when we were all gonna die from climate change.

Since those beauty salons have closed selfies dropped like the stock market.

I'm not adding this year to my age. I didn't use it.

Some days I amaze myself. Other days I look for my phone while I'm talking on it.

Christmas is now gonna be mid-January, due to Santa having to quarantine for 14 days when he arrives in the country.

Can't afford Xmas this year? Just tell your kids Santa is being quarantined at the North Pole.

I need to stay 6 feet away from my debit card. That's really what I need to do.

It took over 70 days of quarantine but we finally got that roll of Christmas wrapping paper from behind the bedroom door put away.

Quarantine Day 158: I've moved on to crocheting car cozies.

It started as a virus but mutated into an IQ test.

I may not have caught the virus but I've managed to catch a few pounds, some anxiety and a taste for social distancing.

My only current hobby and passion is tracking packages.

I Googled my symptoms. Turns out I just need my hair done.

OK, COVID, wrap it up.

I put my symptoms on WebMD and it turns out… I just need to be on a beach with a glass of wine.

June's fighter has entered the ring: CDC warns of aggressive cannibal rats facing shortage of garbage to eat.

I used to wonder what it would be like to read other people's minds. Then I got a Facebook account, and now I'm over it.

Shuffling around your kitchen with Clorox Wipes under your shoes fully counts as mopping. Pass it on.

I gotta be honest: those people from Doomsday Preppers don't really seem that crazy anymore.

Physically, I'm a day away from July. Emotionally, I'm still processing March.

Words I never want to hear again:

- Covid-19
- Social distancing
- Essential worker
- Second wave
- Unprecedented
- Frontline worker
- Flatten the curve
- Stay home, save a life
- Quarantine
- Safer at home
- Dr. Fauci
- Bill Gates
- The science
- We're all in this together
- Mask

We're gonna have to retire the expression "avoid it like the plague" because it turns out humans do not do that.

Relationship status: Slept with the laundry I was too lazy to fold.

Some mornings it's best to just fill the sink with coffee, dunk your head in and suck.

If I ever go missing be sure to use my selfie with the most likes.

My 5 year plan is to make it through this year.

I want to go back to the days when my biggest anxiety was stopping the cassette tape before the DJ started speaking when recording the top 10.

It's Thursday, or as I like to call it: Day 4 of the hostage situation.

Anyone else find yourself momentarily worried about your favorite TV characters when you see them maskless and in one another's bubbles?

Canada must feel like they live in an apartment above a meth lab.

This pandemic is exactly why I hated group projects at school.

My financial status: I just rinsed off a paper plate.

What if this planet is a reality TV show for other planets?

"Once Covid-19 is over" is starting to sound a lot of "when I win the lottery."

Today I tested positive for sickofthis-20. There's no cure and I may or may not be contagious.

You said everything would be back to normal after June. Julyed!

Why are there never any good side effects? Just for once, I'd like to read a medication bottle and see "May cause extreme sexiness."

Do we quarantine until there are no more germs in the world or just until the election is over?

I don't like being in a pandemic with y'all. It's like being on silent lunch but we keep getting days added on because y'all won't shut up.

Let's all Boo 2020 and We're Not Yet Sure About 2021, Either

First rule of 2021: Never talk about 2020

One day 2020 will be the one-word catchphrase for everything messed up and bad. "How's your day?" "A total 2020." "Say no more…"

Good tiding of cheer. To hell with this year.

Does it bother anyone that 2021 is pronounced "2020 won"?

Just wait until 2020 turns 21 and starts drinking…

I'm not wishing anyone "Happy New Year" until at least July when I see how 2021 is going.

No one is writing the wrong year on their checks this January; I can tell you that…

Hear me out: What if 2021 tells 2020 to "Hold my beer"?

What if 2021 is 2020, Version 2.0?

This New Year's Eve remember to drink and wander around your house responsibly.

Maybe it would be good luck, or at least pretty satisfying, if at midnight we all ceremoniously flush our toilets!

We're not doing New Year's resolutions this time. Just keep your head down and your mouth shut until we see what we're working with.

Nobody claim 2021 as "your year". We're all going to walk in real slow. Be good. Be quiet. Don't. Touch. Anything.

Going through 2020 was like going through Kevin's house on Christmas Eve.

Optimist: The glass is half full. Pessimist: The glass is half empty. 2020: That's pee in the glass, isn't it?

I haven't seen any "2021 is gonna be my year" posts yet. You all scared, aren't ya?

Date: December 31, 2020, 11:59 p.m. Congratulations. You have successfully completed the Kobayashi Maru.

I don't need to know the entire plot of 2021. I just need to understand if I should buy skincare and sweatpants or a purse and shoes.

Turning back the clocks and adding an hour to 2020 is like getting a bonus track on a Yoko Ono album.

I'm not turning my clock back on November 1 because seriously none of us need an extra hour of 2020.

Guys, I misplaced my schedule. What day is this week's hurricane supposed to hit?

Don't forget the movie "Reign of Fire" takes place in 2020. So we still have dragons to look forward to.

An extra hour in 2020 is like getting a free appetizer from a restaurant that gave you food poisoning.

I will not be surprised whatsoever if the time goes from 11:59 to 11:60 on New Year's Eve and we become stuck in 2020 forever.

New Christmas tunes for 2020:

- Santa Claus won't be coming to town.
- Rudolph the face-masked reindeer

Accidentally punched myself in the face while trying to pull my blanket up and if that doesn't accurately describe my life in 2020 I don't know what does.

Anyone else concerned about the 2020 season finale?

I think we can stop bragging about having been through the Blizzard of '78. 2020 wins.

Scientists have found that one dog year does not equal 7 human years. In fact, the only thing that equals 7 human years is 2020.

I swear on December 31 ya'll better not say no Happy New Year. Y'all better scream Jumanji so we can get out of this game.

Today marks five years we've been in 2020.

The 12 days of Cor*na In the year 2020, the pandemic gave to me

- 12 canceled plans
- 11 face masks
- 10 squirts of sanitizer
- 9 cases of wine
- 8 friends zooming
- 7 mental breakdowns
- 6 feet apart
- 5 curbside pickups
- 4 Netflix binges
- 3 flights a-cancelled
- 2 bad home haircuts
- And a massive shortage of TP

The 12 Days of Corona. In the year 2020, the pandemic gave to me:

- 12 canceled plans
- 11 face masks
- 10 sanitizers
- 9 murder hornets
- 8 zoom calls
- 7 mental breakdowns
- 6 feet apart
- 5 curbside pickups
- 4 quarantines
- 3 travel restrictions
- 2 Karens complaining
- And a massive shortage of TP.

If 2020 was a math problem: If you're walking on the ice cream at 5 ounces per toaster, and your bicycle loses a sock, how much gravy will you need to repaint your hamster?

So for season 2… I mean the second wave… can we switch quarantine partners or are we stuck with the same ones from season 1?

I've already decided on my Halloween costume for this year… I'm going as the year 2020.

Next time you expect a toddler or a child to share, just remember how adults acted in 2020 over groceries.

I would like to cancel my subscription to the hurricane of the month club, please.

I'm beginning to think that the familiar phrase "hindsight is 2020" originated as a message from a future time traveler that we have always profoundly misunderstood.

Welcome to 2020. If you do not already suffer from an anxiety disorder, one will be assigned to you.

The coin shortage is from people throwing them in fountains wishing 2020 was over.

The Falcons just blew a 20-point lead. At least something normal happened in 2020.

Who has sharks in the power lines on their 2020 bingo card?

Turning back your clocks and getting an extra hour of 2020 is like getting a second helping of sausages and peas in gelatin.

Remember to put your I Voted sticker under your pillow tonight so the election fairy leaves you a Xanax.

2020 should just become a new curse word. I don't give a 2020…

At what point can we just start using 2020 as a swear word? As in: "What a load of 2020." "What the 2020?" "Ab-sa-2020-lutely!"

I have an awesome Beatles calendar for 2020 but it's hard to read because each month has eight days a week.

In the year 2000 they said that we would have colonies on Mars in 20 years. Instead we are watching videos on how to wash our hands.

Is four a lot? Depends upon the context. Dollars, no. Days without a disaster in 2020? Yes.

Before: Goodyear After: Badyear

This year, the Harvest moon won't arrive until October 1. That means October gets two full moons—the other is a Blue Moon, occurring on Halloween, October 31. Who had double werewolves for October?

2020: Weddings: 10 people. Funerals: 10 people. Protests: 1,000 people.

In 2019 everyone used that aging app to see how they'd look when they were old, but it was really how you'll look at the end of 2020.

At 11:59 December 31 we all gotta take a shot and never speak of this year EVER AGAIN

I can't believe we stayed up and screamed "Happy New Year" for this mess.

You're planning for next year? That's cute.

I'm going to stay up on New Year's Eve this year. Not to see the New Year in, but to make sure this one leaves.

2020: The year my trash bin went out more than me.

2021: "I know what you did last summer." 2020: "Not a %^&* thing!"

So anyone want to take bets on 2021? Volcano? Locusts? Asteroids? New Nickleback album?

Prediction for 2020: Bermuda Triangle just starts roaming around the earth slowly like a Roomba.

Other people: What did you learn from Quarantine 2020? Me: Bigfoot's name is Darryl.

We need Samuel Jackson to narrate 2020. No offense to Morgan Freeman, but this year requires multiple uses for the word MF.

A man walks into a bar and orders a Corona and two Hurricanes. The bartender says "That'll be $20.20."

13: "I am the worst number!" 666: "No, I am!" 2020: "Ha ha ha ha!"

Coming up in August 2020: Killer tomatoes!

Hurricanes Laura and Marco are the official couple of 2020.

2020 has given us a hot mess of a year so far and now hurricanes in the south! What's next… Release the Kraken?

Being 20 in the seventies was much more fun than being 70 in the twenties.

If 2020 was a drink, what would it be? Colonoscopy prep.

If 2020 was a drink, it would be the Orange Glucose Tolerance Test drink.

Wrote a song called 2020. It goes something like this: "AAAAAAAAAAAAAAAAAAAAH!"

The most useless button of 2020: Airplane mode.

What if 2020 is just a trailer for 2021?

We should stop making memes about 2020 getting worse. It seems to listen to us.

How December 2020 is going to look: Merry Crisis and a Happy New Fear

Scientists have found that one dog year does not equal seven human years. In fact, the only thing that equals seven human years is 2020.

If 2020 was a piñata it would be a wasp's nest.

Who had "Double Hurricanes" on their 2020 bingo card?

(photo of 20 reams of paper between book covers): Well, that didn't work. A brief history of 2020.

Remember that one girl from high school that said she'd only go out with you if the world was ending? Well, this may be the year to give her a call.

Dear 2020: First of all, I would like you let you know I'm typing this with my middle finger.

If 2020 were a math problem: If you're going down a river at 2 MPH and your canoe loses a wheel, how much pancake mix would you need to re-shingle your roof?

I'm not buying a 2021 planner until I see a trailer.

To clarify, when I asked for two hurricanes, I was referring to the drink.

Maybe 2020 will be like a mullet, and we party on the back half of it.

The worst part of 2020 ain't even here yet. If Hurricane Nana reaches Category 5 she's gonna make us pick our own hickory switch.

So I just figured out 2020 and it's pretty obvious what happened: "Baby Shark" is an ancient chant that opens a portal to Hell.

Flirting in 2020 be like: Blink if you want me!

Computer: End program "2020" and delete file.

Coping: Some Good, Some Maybe Not the Best Coping Mechanisms

I need to get my life together but I'm kind of waiting to see if the world's going to end before I put any real effort in.

I know Amazon drivers be like "dang, this house again!"

During the lockdown, I've run out of entertainment. So I send David, my neighbor, flowers every Saturday evening with a message, "I miss you." Then I go to my balcony with a drink and listen to his wife.

Today's forecast: Lazy with a chance of Netflix.

I used to think my parents did pizza and a movie on Friday nights to be fun but now I know they were just tired.

Hey, Debbie? It's me, the Lord. Listen, you need to stop telling Facebook that your health is in My hands. You're going to have to wash your hands and quarantine with everyone else. OK?

I still don't know what I am wearing to the living room for Thanksgiving. I might not go.

I still don't know what I'm wearing to the living room New Year's Eve… I might not even go.

Siri, how do I always mess it up with women? Um, this is Alexa.

Rapunzel was quarantined and met her future husband. So let's think positively here.

If I flirted with you this year, it doesn't count. I thought we were about to die.

The CDC suggests washing your hands for the length of a song. In A Gadda Da Vida is not the song.

Please satanize your hands here.

Doctor: How often do you exercise? Me: 3 times. Doctor: A week? A month? Me: I have given my answer.

If anyone is alone with no family or nobody to spend Thanksgiving with please let me know! I need to borrow some chairs.

Yesterday I saw a book called "How to Solve Half of Your Problems". So I bought two.

Who had zombie Covid minks on their bingo card?

Whenever I am asked to do something I don't want to: I answer, "In a pandemic?" It's worked pretty well so far.

Sir, we need to take your temperature before entering the store. Ma'am, have you ever seen a man with a fever, walking?

Quarantine day? Today I melted an ice cube with my mind just by staring at it. It took a lot longer than I thought it would.

When the world is about to end, I hope we know about it in advance so I can stop doing laundry.

If we are in lockdown for Christmas. Remember this is NOT the government's fault. It's the Public's Fault! This is your 9 week warning! Wear a mask. Wash your hands. Follow the guidelines. Stop spreading the virus. Don't ruin it for everyone else.

Wanna hear a coronavirus joke? Sure. Not gonna tell ya. You might spread it.

[Having to cough out in public] Excuse me everyone. I need to inform you that I do Not have the Covid. I simply have choked on my own spit because I am truly incompetent as a human.

Sometimes all you need is a good nap and like 5 million dollars.

Philadelphia police arrested 57 cardboard cutouts after leaving the stadium for fighting.

When leaving the house. 2019: Keys, phone, wallet. 2020: Keys, phone, wallet, mask, hand sanitizer, written will, hornet repellent, protest sign, goggles, body armor, leaf blower.

Leaving the house in 2019: keys, phone, purse, water Leaving the house in 2020: keys, phone, purse, water, face mask, hand sanitizer, latex gloves, holy water, wooden stake, full medieval body armor

The fact that jellyfish have survived for 650 million years despite not having brains gives hope to many people.

No Money November was a success. Dead Broke December is about to be poppin'!

Be sure to bring up politics at Thanksgiving this year, to save on Christmas gifts.

Happy 6 month anniversary to "14 days to flatten the curve"

One day you will tell your story of how you've overcome what you're going through now, and it will become part of someone else's survival guide.

To all you panic shoppers: Please stock up on condoms so you don't reproduce more idiots...

During this trying time, I have been able to take bad news in stride; but if I find one more spoon with peanut butter all over it in the dishwasher I cannot be responsible for what happens next.

Fencing: The Perfect Covid-19 Sport. Masks. Gloves. If anyone gets closer than six feet to you, you stab them.

Maybe if we all sit real still, 2020 won't be able to see us.

Welcome, Campers. Safe Social Distancing

- Bears: 100 yards
- Skunks: 50 yards
- Raccoons 25 yards
- Aunt Edna: 6 feet

Sweet Baby Jesus: Please make BBQ the cure for coronavirus.

I feel like if cicadas are allowed to just sit in a tree and scream I should also be.

Shelter-in-place coping levels as measured in cartoon bears

1. Level 1: Berenstain. Fully clothed, family unit all together, societal rules and standards still being followed, practiced, and respected.

2. Level 2: Pooh. T-shirt and no pants, mostly alone, eating entirely too many sweets but happy in your blissful ignorance.

3. Level 3: Yogi. Naked except for a hat and tie, surviving off whatever food you can steal, only companion is a smaller nude person in a bow tie.

4. Level 4: Charmin. Completely nude, surrounded by others who are completely nude, obsessed with toilet paper.

Due to recent events, morning screaming hours have been extended indefinitely.

Quarantine Month 3: Roomba battles

My wife didn't order anything from Amazon yesterday so the UPS guy knocked on our door to see if we're ok.

Finally shaved my legs and donated it to Locks of Love.

I was out shopping and pretended that the one-way arrows on the floor were speed boosts. So it only made sense to drop bananas behind me, thus slowing the other racers while also ensuring maximum social distancing by chucking cans of soup at them.

If you keep a margarita in one hand and some tacos in the other hand you will never touch your face. Follow me on more tips on how to stay safe during the pandemic.

For your safety, due to the carnivorous, we will not be able to open the pool this season.

Does anyone know if there are special looting hours for seniors?

Hate when Walmart doesn't have what I need and I have to go home, change out of my pajamas and brush my hair so I can go to Target.

So small talk will be banned in hairdressers in new Covid guidelines. I might actually go and get my hair done now.

I feel that I should clean the house so I am heading out to the garden until that feeling passes.

Person: Do you just look at memes all day without socializing? Me: It's a peaceful life.

University of Facebook School of Medicine: Have you ever wanted to practice medicine without all the hassle of being responsible for people dying? Well, here at University of Facebook School of Medicine our motto is "Anyone can be a Doctor". Our most popular courses include "Why face masks don't work" followed by my personal favorite "Masks are unhealthy and cause you to get sick". Don't let your lack of medical training or experience stop you from posting bad medical advice. Our online courses are not limited by classroom size and best of all no enrollment fees or intelligence is required. So enroll now and start your career as an unqualified Facebook doctor today!

People must not cough near you. They must cough far away. If you hear someone coughing, tell them to… far cough.

Worried about getting COVID-19 from a gas pump? Use a cigarette lighter to burn the virus off the nozzle before you fuel up. You'll be immune to the virus the rest of your life.

Hugh Hefner became a multi millionaire staying home in his jammies. I'm not having the same result.

Do you suffer from astral plane sex with demons? Ask your "doctor" if hydroxychloroquine is right for you.

(photo of Daft Punk in their spaceman helmets): Choral Director concert wardrobe 2020

One minute you're young and free and the next minute you're super-excited that your grocery pickup order had no substitutions or out of stock items.

At this point, Jesus doesn't need to take the wheel… He needs to pull over and spank some of y'all with his flip-flop.

Travel—Not!

Me if I crash on a deserted island this year: DON'T SEND HELP

Congrats, America! 51 years ago, we walked on the moon. Now we can't even go to Canada.

Dear airlines: Please stop emailing me deals unless you can give me a nonstop flight from my couch to my kitchen. Thanks.

I can't wait to walk down the aisle someday... and hear those magical words... "This is your pilot speaking."

If Trump wins I am leaving the country. If Biden wins I am leaving the country. This is not a political post. I just want to travel.

My husband purchased a world map...gave me a dart and said "throw this and wherever it lands I'm taking you for a holiday when this pandemic is over." Turns out we're spending two weeks behind the fridge.

Calculate Your Next Travel Destination

1. Choose a number between 1 and 9
2. Multiply it by 3
3. Add 3
4. Multiply by 3 again
5. Add the two digits together
6. The number you're left with is where you're traveling to!

    1. Japan
    2. Hawaii
    3. Paris
    4. Bali
    5. Australia
    6. Barbados
    7. Italy
    8. Kenya
    9. Stay home
    10. Cuba
    11. New York
    12. Jamaica
    13. Greece
    14. Thailand
    15. The Maldives

Boredom

Some people are solving major world problems, and I'm over here all excited because I found my missing sock inside a pair of my underwear.

First, coffee. Then we move on to today's episode of "Now what?"

8 a.m.: Too tired to think. Noon: Too tired to think. 5 p.m.: Too tired to think. Midnight: How do dragons blow out candles?

Due to my isolation, I finished three books yesterday. And believe me, that's a lot of coloring.

Kevin McCallister gave us unrealistic expectations about how much fun it is to be home alone.

How bored are you? I don't skip YouTube ads.

Remember overscheduling yourself and your family to the brink of physical and mental collapse? Man, those were the days.

I hate when people ask me what I did yesterday. I don't know. I breathed a lot. Probably got mad at something... Sighed heavily. The list goes on.

We all have a favorite eyebrow.

You only live once, so make sure you spend 7 hours a day scrolling on social media!

Someone just used my driveway to turn around and now I'm standing outside with two open beers and a lonely face.

Not sure what everyone else is doing today, but if you're not painting your chicken's toenails, are you really living your best life?

Through weeks of quarantine Fluffy had picked up some bad habits from his human. Binge watching Tiger King was one…

You ever go on YouTube just to watch a music video and then 5 hours later you finding yourself watching a tutorial on how to talk to a giraffe?

I say we go back to using Facebook for what we originally used it for: looking up exes to see how fat they got.

Sitting in your car outside of your house is self-care. I can't explain it but if you know you know.

Hobby Drinking

During the Middle Ages, they celebrated the end of the plague with wine and orgies. Does anyone know if they had anything like that planned when this one ends? (Asking for a friend)

I'll have a café mocha vodka valium latte to go, please.

Is it ok to pull the bag of wine out of the box and stab a straw in it like it's a giant Capri Sun? Asking for a friend.

Do not drink and wrap presents. Also, if anyone gets a remote control for Christmas, I'm gonna need that back.

Pfft. The liquor store clerk wished me a Merry Christmas as if he wasn't going to see me 14 more times before then.

Dear liver: This month will be rough. Stay strong.

"Drink, drank, drunk" is the 2020 version of "live, laugh, love".

I just tried to make my own hand sanitizer and it came out as a margarita.

It's not drinking alone if the cat's home.

People who wonder if the glass is half empty or half full miss the point. The glass is refillable.

How much should you spend on a bottle of wine? I don't know… half an hour?

Education is important, but opening the pubs is importanter.

Not to get technical… but according to chemistry, alcohol is a solution.

I'm giving up drinking till Christmas. Sorry, bad punctuation. I'm giving up. Drinking till Christmas.

No longer 5 o'clock somewhere. It's 2020 everywhere. Drink when you want.

I'm giving up drinking until this is over. Sorry, bad punctuation. I'm giving up. Drinking until this is over.

Today I was a hero! I rescued some beer that was trapped in a bottle.

And then alcohol said, "Post that on Facebook. It's hilarious." But alcohol was wrong. So very wrong.

Bars are closed. We should all go drink in the woods like we used to.

Dear Bartender: Don't be offended if we ask "Is there any liquor in this drink?" Please remember we've been making our own for the last 9 weeks. Just sayin'…

I have a feeling my Check Liver light might come on this weekend.

Every weekend I say to myself, "Susan, you have to stop drinking wine." Thankfully, I'm not Susan.

I can hose down a lot more margaritas than I could pre-pandemic. What does that say about me?

I started jogging today. I didn't want to, but the margarita truck didn't stop.

My doctor has given me three days to give up drinking. I've picked June 5, July 17 and October 9.

I ran twice today. First, I ran out of beer, and then I ran to get some more.

Trust me, you can dance! --Vodka

Sometimes I take a bath because it's harder to drink a glass of wine in the shower.

Me: Alexa, remind me to go to the gym. Alexa: I have added gin to your shopping list.

Someone offered me grapes and I declined. I'm not going to consume wine in pill form.

If you have to choose between drinking wine every day and being skinny, which would you choose? Red or white?

I ain't getting coronavirus. I drink Budweiser.

Does anyone know which page of the Bible explains how to turn water into wine? Asking for a friend.

I tried to login to my iPad. Turns out it was an Etch-a-Sketch and I don't own an iPad. Also, I'm out of wine.

Me: Please bring me a screwdriver. Wife: Flat head, Phillips, or Vodka? And that was when I knew she was the one.

Everyday Covid check: At 5 p.m., open a bottle of wine, smell it, then pour it into a glass. If you can smell it and taste it, you are good. Celebrate by finishing the bottle. You are welcome!

Everyday Covid check: At 7 p.m., open the whiskey bottle and smell it. If you can smell, you are not affected. Then pour it into a glass. Taste it. If you can feel the taste, you are definitely not affected. –Dr. Johnny Walker

Self-testing for Covid-19. Pour a measure of whiskey, gin, or rum into a glass, then see if you can smell it. If you can, then drink it and if you can taste it it's reasonable to assume you are currently free of the virus. I tested myself nine times last night and was virus-free each time, thank Goodness. I will test myself again today because I have developed a headache which can also be a symptom.

I just got pulled over by the cops. He said, "I can smell alcohol." I told him that's because you're not respecting social distancing.

Hobby Eating

Day One: Meditation, yoga, smoothie for breakfast. Day Four: *pours ice cream over pasta*

Day 12 without chocolate: lost hearing in my left eye

Every time I try to eat healthy, along comes Thanksgiving, Christmas, Summer, Friday, or Tuesday and it ruins it for me.

Shout out to everyone who said they would start eating healthy in the new year and already decided to wait until Monday.

My goal for 2020 was to lose 10 pounds. Only 14 more to go.

It's all fun and games until your oversized shirts start fitting.

I just realized that if I want to reach my goal weight by New Year's Day, I should have stopped eating and drinking in 2005!

Eat like nobody is going to see you naked.

Managing your weight around the holidays just requires a little planning… For example, I took the batteries out of my scale last Wednesday.

I need to get back in shape but I'm kind of waiting to see if the world is going to end before I put any real effort in.

When you think about how huge the Earth is, and how the Earth is just a tiny ball orbiting the Sun, which in turn is a minuscule spec in the universe… It's pretty easy to rationalize eating an entire pie.

I don't have an Advent calendar so I'm just opening cupboard doors and eating whatever's in there.

I was gonna start dieting, but Halloween is coming up, then Thanksgiving and Christmas candy. Before you know it, it's BBQ season again and I'm not about to turn down a cheeseburger.

Anyone else starting to get a tan from the light in your refrigerator?

Anyone else feel like Halloween is unnecessary this year? I've been wearing a mask and eating candy for 7 months now. I don't think I need a day dedicated to it any more.

I'm not sure how many cookies it takes to be happy, but so far it's not 27.

I just ate what I thought was a feta cheese crumble from my salad off my shirt. Turns out it was deodorant. So, how's your day going?

Breaking news: Wearing a mask inside your home is now highly recommended. Not so much to prevent Covid-19 but to stop eating.

Dear Santa, All I want is a fat bank account and a skinny body. Please don't mix it up again like last year.

Top Three things I gained so far from 2020:

1. Weight
2.
3.

There should be a calorie refund for things that didn't taste as good as you expected.

Does anyone know where adults can trick or treat? Looking for a neighborhood that hands out tacos and margaritas.

Things I need to stay 6 feet away from: Refrigerator, Mexican food, debit card, Amazon

I had a date last night. Really enjoyed it. So tonight I'm going to try a fig.

Accidentally went grocery shopping on an empty stomach and now I'm the proud owner of aisle 4.

Gardening season is off to a great start: I planted myself in front of a TV four weeks ago, and I've already grown noticeably.

If a woman asks if she is Fat, it's not enough to say no. You must Always act very surprised by the question. Jump Backwards If Necessary.

Unfortunately Thanksgiving is canceled this year due to Covid. Sadly our pet turkey has passed away and we are holding a visitation. In lieu of flowers please bring a salad… or a side dish.

Six allowed at Thanksgiving but 30 at a funeral. I will be holding a funeral for my pet turkey that will pass away on November 26. Refreshments provided.

Can you imagine how sexy I would be if I ate right and took care of my body? I mean… I'm not going to, but can you imagine?

Here's the problem with fruit: It's inconsistent. Some apples are delicious, some taste bad. Sometimes blueberries are great, sometimes they are disgusting. You know what's the same every time? Doritos

It amazes me how much exercise and extra fries sound alike.

Listen, frozen meal instructions: Never in the history of owning microwaves have I known the wattage of any microwave.

I go outside every few days just to make sure I still fit through the door.

Doing crunches twice a day now. Captain in the morning. Nestle in the afternoon.

Photo of me, eating a $7 sandwich that cost me $45 on Uber Eats.

I just had a physical. The doctor said, "Don't eat anything fatty." I said, "Like bacon and burgers?" He said, "No, fatty, don't eat anything!"

I have decided to avoid everything that makes me fat… pictures, mirrors, and scales.

Just before quarantine, when you ordered a cake you knew it had to be somebody's birthday. These days, I find myself wondering why I've wasted so much of my life NOT eating straight out of the can on a daily basis.

When you're at the checkout line and they ask you if you found everything, say, "Why, are you hiding stuff?"

I did a push-up today. Well, actually, I fell down. But I had to use my arms to get back up so… you know, close enough. I need some chocolate.

The 19 after COVID is the average amount of weight gained during lockdown.

I don't get how shows like Iron Chef and Chopped became so popular. They're all "make something out of this random ingredient". That's how I make dinner every night and it's not that exciting.

I have asked Publix to put Xs at both ends of the candy and cookie aisles since I've lost my willpower.

Some people say your body is a temple. Mine is a bounce castle.

I never would have believed that a few weeks of uncut hair would weigh 20 pounds but that's what the scale says.

Somebody asked me what to do with left over bacon. I've never heard of that kind of bacon. Is it new?

What if they close grocery stores and we have to hunt our own food? I don't even know where Little Debbie lives.

Dear sweet baby Jesus: Please don't make Brussels sprouts the cure for coronavirus.

Lockdown can only go four ways. You'll come out a monk, a hunk, a chunk, or a drunk. Choose wisely.

Currently standing in front of my pantry eating a "temporary" snack while trying to decide on a more formal, permanent snack.

How long do you keep a pair of jeans that you hope you can fit back into one day? It's 30 years, right?

Does the jelly in a donut count as a serving of fruit? Asking for a friend.

If I was Snow White you'd never be able to keep me with an apple... you'd have to poison an éclair or something...

I'm about 5 pounds away from Google Maps listing me as a roundabout.

Once you realize you don't need a special occasion to buy a cake, the second part of your life begins.

It's strange how drinking 8 cups of water seems impossible but 8 cups of coffee go down like a chubby kid on a see-saw.

If it is true that stress brings on weight loss, why the heck am I not invisible?

I just dropped a pack of M&Ms into my mask at work and am slowly eating them like a horse. I love the pandemic.

I hate brushing my teeth at night because that signifies that you can't have any more food and I'm just never ready for that kind of commitment.

"Just a little midnight snack," I whisper, knowing full well I have no concept of what time it is, what day it is, or what the words "little snack" even mean.

My friend: "OMG, do you want to do a triathlon with me?" Me: "OMG, want to try all the new Lay's potato chip flavors with me?"

Me: Could you grow, please? Hair: Nope. Muscles: Nope. Stomach: I got you.

A salad is a great thing to eat when you're hungry… and want to stay that way.

You can leave $5,000 unattended in a room with me and every dime is gonna be there. Now if you leave M&Ms or something, that's your fault.

Two things to make your day better. 1. Do not watch the news. 2. Stay off the bathroom scales.

I'm so offended when my body decides to be sick. Like I gave you a vegetable last week. How dare you?

The two types of people in quarantine: Person One: I ran ten miles this morning. Person Two: I'm trying to figure out how to stuff ice cream into pancakes.

Warning: Some supermarkets are scanning your forehead as you try to enter their shop claiming they're taking your temperature. It's a lie. They're wiping your memory… I went to the shop for salad, chicken, and some low calorie dressing and left with crisps, chocolate, and alcohol!

Do you have any idea how hard it is to eat my secret stash of potato chips in a house with five kids who never leave?

Experts: A serving size of chips is 10 chips. Actual Humans: I eat 10 chips while I'm standing in the pantry with the bag open, trying to decide if I want to eat chips.

"Enjoy yourself while you can" Thanks for the anxiety, fortune cookie.

I'm not sure if going to a Mexican restaurant and eating 7 baskets of chips and salsa is going to solve any of my problems but there's only one way to find out.

Keep in mind, even during a pandemic, no matter how much chocolate you eat, your earrings will still fit.

Look y'all… COVID is like eating raw cookie dough. I know the risk. Now just let me live my life.

We're all brave in our own way. For example, I'm not afraid to eat raw cookie dough.

Quarantine tip: Your pants won't be too tight if you don't wear any.

If you weigh 200 pounds on Earth, you'll be only 76 pounds on Mars. You're not overweight, you're just not on the right planet.

At first I thought I had COVID because I couldn't breathe. Then I unbuttoned my pants and it was all ok.

Once you accept the fact that queso and margaritas taste better than being skinny, the second half of your life begins.

Good morning to everyone except people who don't gain weight when they eat whatever they want. I hate y'all.

The sad moment you lose a chip in the dip so you send in a recon chip and that breaks, too.

Remember when there weren't enough Popeye's Chicken sandwiches and that was a crisis? Good times.

Pretty weird how we are all now living in a time when not going to the gym is considered healthy.

I don't know who needs to hear this, but you can eat peach cobbler any time of day.

My favorite game is trying to take something out of the refrigerator without moving the other items in front of it. I call it Refrigerator Jenga, and when you lose you clean up marinara for 40 minutes.

Who Needs The Hunt for Red October When We've Got The Hunt for Toilet Paper?

(Picture of duct tape) You haven't truly experienced toilet paper until you have enjoyed it in the original Klingon.

Toilet Paper shortage might be due to the fact that teachers can now use the bathroom whenever they want.

(Photo of hewn logs) Do not order toilet paper from Ikea.

I just realized that someone replaced the toilet paper roll. I'm now concerned that there is someone living here that I don't know.

Hurricane season is next. Are all y'all crazy toilet paper people gonna buy all the light bulbs in case the power goes out?

To all you Numb Nuts that are hoarding all the toilet paper: I'm buying up all the plungers. Checkmate.

For Hanukkah 2020: The "Toilet Paper Menorah" to remind us of the time that we had 1 roll of toilet paper but we made it last for 8 days and 8 nights.

Whatever happens, please don't buy all the freaking toilet paper again.

I recently bought a toilet brush… Long story short, I'm going back to toilet paper.

I wonder if I throw a roll of toilet paper in the middle of the Walmart parking lot if people will attack it like seagulls fighting over French fries.

Have you been traumatized by the toilet paper shortage? You may be entitled to constipation.

I still can't believe that people's survival instincts told them to grab toilet paper.

Corona Precautions: I went to the bathroom at a restaurant. I washed my hands. Opened the door with my elbow. Raised the toilet seat with my foot. I switched on the water faucet with a tissue. Opened the bathroom door to leave with my elbow. And when I returned to my table I realized… I forgot to pull up my pants!

Dear shoppers: Due to the recent outbreak of STUPIDITY and Panic-Purchasing by complete idiots, the nation is currently experiencing a shortage of toilet paper and common sense. Expect supplies to be replenished once these sheep-minded morons have all starved to death in their homes, surrounded by toilet paper but without anything to eat.

I don't care how nice the hand soap smells. You should never walk out of the restroom sniffing your fingers.

I know it was months ago, but I still don't like how you all acted over toilet paper.

For those who fantasize about living in a different time period: toilet paper was not invented until 1880.

In 20 years when kids ask about the 2020 toilet paper shortage, I'm telling them we had to drag our butts across the lawn, in the snow, uphill, both ways, while dodging murder hornets.

Homeschooling, Distance Learning, and Traditional School

It turns out that when you're asked who your favorite child is, you're supposed to pick one of your own. I know that now.

This homeschool thing wouldn't be so bad if we had a better janitor.

It takes a village to raise a kid. It takes a distillery to home school one.

Homeschooling Day 4: It's pretty awkward when I suspend a student, but still have to make them dinner.

Homeschooling Day 4: Considering texting students in the middle of instruction with parents… just so they get the full effect.

Covid-19: Crushing the dreams of children everywhere as they watch their teachers become YouTubers before they do.

Parents seeing a school bus in 2020 is the equivalent of a kid seeing an ice cream truck in the summer.

Do anybody else kids be walking around the house "Skipping Class" right in front of you?

Today's geography lesson is tracking Mommy's Amazon package.

I remember asking my teachers when I would ever need the math they were teaching me. Not one, not a single one of them, said I would need it to teach to my son during a plague.

Really don't get people freaking out over online school like "My child is falling behind! His education is suffering!" Education for what? Half my friends are bartenders with masters' degrees. Your kind could spend a year learning to make different quiches and come out ahead.

My husband walked into our closet to find me drinking a large coffee and eating a doughnut in the dark. He said, "Do the kids know you are in here?" To which I replied, "Welcome to the teachers' lounge."

Husband: What are all these Amazon packages? Me: Oh, that's a gift for the homeschool teacher? Husband: So… you? Me: Yep. And this one is for the kids' chauffeur. This one is for the baby's wet nurse. Oh and this is for the cleaning lady. Husband: So everything is for you? Me: Yep.

When I feel my patience running low with the 6-year-old lately (which is often these days) I try to remember that one day in March, without warning, we picked him up from school and then he never saw his friends again and even most adults would lack the tools to process that.

There's no crying in remote learning.

I'm not sure how my child will survive back at school without 6 breakfasts, 2 lunches, and 3,546 snacks during the day.

The devil whispered to the homeschool mom, "Your not strong enough to withstand this storm." She whispered back, "You're."

Online class: Elementary vs. High School

Elementary School

OK, settle down, everyone.
My chair fell over!
My Dog is here!
AM I ON MUTE?
And here's my room…
This is my Dad's shoe!

High school

Can anyone say good morning? Anyone?

A skill I never expected to see on our son's kindergarten report card: Can independent mute and unmute himself when requested to do so.

It's the last week of school and I'm proud to say that my husband and I have a B- in 3rd grade math.

10-year-old: Ugh. Why do I have to do all this stupid work? Me: So you can one day become a brilliant scientist who discovers cures for viruses and saves parents from having to homeschool.

It may take a village to raise a child, but it's going to take a vineyard to homeschool one.

Senior skip day record goes to the class of 2020

Dear Zoom, Thanks for being there for me during a crisis, but it's time to break up. Also, it's not me, it's you. Sincerely, Educators

When Alice Cooper sang, "School's out forever", I didn't take him for a prophet.

PSA: Don't EVER let your printer know that you've waited until the last minute to print something out and you're in a hurry because they can sense fear.

So, your kids can figure out Instagram, Snapchat, Tik Tok, and Twitter. They can spend 8+ hours a day on a video game until they beat the whole thing, but they can't figure out how to upload an assignment to Google Classroom? Interesting. Please tell me more.

Parents: Don't forget you can't leave your students alone so you can go to the bathroom. Find coverage or hold it.

I just sent all the children to their rooms and changed the computer password, in case anyone wondered how today is going…

Do you know what profession would last the longest in the zombie apocalypse? Teachers. Because they already knew how to survive with little to no resources.

Sure, I could parent without screen time. I could also churn my own butter but let's not get crazy here.

2020: The year parents officially stopped saying "They grow up so fast."

Fathers of students: Please wear shirts while I'm live chatting your child. Thanks.

I can't believe that school used to start at 8 a.m. and I actually went.

Since y'all are at home, please take this time to homeschool yourselves on the differences between "your" and "you're" and "their", "there", and "they're".

Now that school will be closed for a while, my kids will be taking:

- AP chores
- Honors yard work
- Dishwashing 101
- AP Trash Disposal
- Home Economics, aka make your own lunch
- Honors Laundry

How I feel about Covid home school: My Mom let me graduate grades 4-12 in one week!

(photo of kid in pajamas): School pictures this year

What math problems will look like this year: If the CDC recommends that students sit 6 feet apart, and Ms. Johnson's classroom is 500 square feet, calculate how long it will take for people to realize that 25 kids do NOT fit in there?

The look on teachers' faces when the CDC says that schools need to have enough hand sanitizer, paper towels, tissues, and other supplies teachers have been requesting for years.

Your kid's stomach ain't hurt one time since school's been out. Pay attention.

English teachers on Facebook must feel the same hopelessness that dentists do when they're at a candy shop.

Study finds parents can do 1/3 of their kids' maths, but struggle with the other ¾.

When you tell a struggling parent to "enjoy every moment", it's like telling someone with a migraine to "be thankful they have a head" and neither is helpful, okay?

So are we buying school clothes in August or pajamas? Asking for myself…

How am I supposed to give my students "The Look" with a mask on?

Pretty sure this is what they would call a teachable moment: Just in: More than 40 South Bay school principals are in quarantine after being exposed to Covid-19 during an in-person meeting to plan the reopening of schools.

So our plan for reopening school in the fall hinges on students practicing proper hygiene at all times? We are doomed.

First day of school procedures: Place your homework in the bank-like pneumatic tube and hit Send. It will travel to my desk where I will grade and return to you. Do not leave your seat and please do NOT put your mask in the tube! Friendly reminder: no name, no grade! Do not send me your pencil to sharpen, use your hand held.

Admin in 2020: Please be prepared to teach online, in person, both simultaneously, on a moving train, while juggling, in a burning building, under the sea, during a wrestling match with a T-Rex, as a hologram, and riding a unicorn. Also be safe and we value you.

... Have y'all met Children? Opinion: schools can reopen safely if students wear masks and socially distance.

If they put a marching band director in charge of this crisis, it would be over. Everyone would keep their spacing and no one would be touching their face.

Some call it "distance learning". Others refer to it as "remote teaching". I like to call it "long distance email troubleshooting, mixed with a bowlful of excessive videoconferences, deep fried in a vat of 'mute your mics'".

So much to do. So little desire to do it.

What teachers need to unwind on summer break: a secluded beach, and a never-ending supply of margaritas. What teachers can afford on their salary: an inflatable swimming pool and box wine.

Schools can't even control lice. You really trust them to control Covid?

"Not plugging in the kids' tablet" is the new "forgetting to thaw the chicken for dinner" and is a punishable offense.

I've been having my kid water our fake plants with a spray bottle. It keeps him entertained for the exact amount of time it takes me to drink a hot cup of coffee. I have no regrets.

Friend: "Oh, is your kid 4? Mine was reading at 4." Me: "Cool. Mine knows every word to 'Baby Got Back'".

Newest tee-shirt: World's okayest homeschool teacher!

Kids next year after being homeschooled: "But my momma said she wrote the Declaration of Independence!"

Now is the time for teachers to eat: Quit your job and charge $250/week to home school 10 kids. Do such a great job that we never send these kids back to school. Your class of 25 students will be cut to 10 and your income goes from $30,000 to $130,000. You're welcome.

"Don't lick the desk!" Just another Monday.

COVID-19 should be called the Common Core Virus because none of the math is adding up.

Pretty much when I got up on Saturday morning and watched six straight hours of cartoons, my parents didn't feel half the guilt I do when my kids get up and do the same thing.

People posting "you have no excuse for your house not being clean after this quarantine" statuses obviously aren't trapped indoors with their womb gremlins.

Sometimes I wonder if I'm teaching my 2-year-old daughter everything she'll need to be a strong, successful woman. But then I handed her a baby wipe and she used it to wash her armpits. So we're good.

I've been teaching for 10 years, but three of those were in middle school. So technically I've been teaching for 28 years, because one year of middle school ages you like 7 years. It's like dog years.

School Supplies: 3 limes, 1 box of #2 pencils, Margarita mix, 4 glue sticks—clear, Margarita salt, 10 pack of crayons, 3 bottles of Tequila, safety scissors

(Photo of girl walking down the street alone, playing flute): Homeschool marching band

E-learning in progress. Please do not ring bell unless you have wine or teach math.

You're going to send your kid to school with the Paw Patrol mask and he's going to come home with a Spider Man mask because he made a trade at lunch. The whole school will be shut down the next day.

Anyone who thinks children won't purposefully lick their hands and chase each other yelling "Corona" has never met children.

You know you've had a long day of parenting when you hear a mysterious creaking on the floorboards after bedtime and you pray it's a ghost and not your kids getting out of bed again.

There is nothing more disheartening than pretending to sleep next to your toddler for what feels like an eternity, hoping they finally fell asleep and then opening your eyes only to see them staring right at you like a serial killer.

Let me say this loud for those in the back: Teachers are not responsible for the recovery of the economy, babysitting children, or "getting us back to normal". Stop trying to guilt us into risking our lives for the government's failure to act.

Neighbor: "Hi, buddy. How you doing this morning?" My 3-year-old: "Good. My mom puts heavy things on me at night so I can't move or get out of bed." Me: A weighted blanket. We gave him a weighted blanket.

Barista: How do you like your coffee? Me: without kids.

When parents start to crack during lockdown: "Mom, am I adopted?" "No, not yet. I only put the ad out yesterday."

Working From Home

I was working part-time and got fired. It was a full-time job.

I wonder what the part of my brain that used to remember phone numbers is up to these days.

I think we need to stop calling it "working from home" and start calling it "living at work".

I don't accept video calls after 8 p.m. because my face has been restored back to factory settings.

Life is now just a series of uncomfortable Zoom meetings separated by snacks.

Blowing on the wine in your coffee mug will help convince the rest of the Zoom people that your tea is hot.

Quote of the year 2020: "You're on mute!"

You are not stuck at home. You are safe at home.

Nothing annoys me more than a social function that requires pants wearing and shirt tucking.

Covido, ergo Zoom. –Rene Descartes

Virtual meetings are basically modern séances. "Elizabeth, are you here?" "Make a sound if you can hear us." "Is anyone else with you?" "We can't see you. Can you hear us?"

All of these Zoom meetings are making me feel bad about my neck and my chins…

Do all your Zoom meetings sound like Romper Room? I see Billy, Bobby, Sally, and Suzie.

If Zoom would go ahead and add a makeup filter that would be great.

If you could end the corona outbreak by sacrificing an app, what app would you choose and why Zoom?

I want my house just clean enough, so that when people come over unexpectedly, it doesn't look like we're 5 days into battling a poltergeist.

Shoutout to everyone who got through the day without taking a nap. Pulled an all-dayer today. Pretty tough.

Remember how Jane Jetson had a mask for her video telephone calls? I need one of those for my Zoom meetings!

I might sleep on the couch to cut down on my morning commute.

Why do I feel compelled to Wave at the end of Zoom calls? I have literally never walked out of a meeting room Waving!

My 2nd grader has 5 video meetings per day. Five. At one point he says, "I think this one could have been an email." So I guess he's ready for the corporate world.

Social Distancing

We all have that one friend that we can't put on speaker phone because we have no idea what the hell is going to come out of their mouth.

Social Distance Cookie Exchange 2020: Everyone comes by my house and leaves cookies on my porch. There's no exchange. I just eat all the cookies. Follow me for more holiday ideas.

I need some sort of away message for texts that says something like: "Hi! I am exhausted from human interaction. I know I am posting on social media, but I currently just don't have energy to hold a conversation. I still love you, and will get back to you in 3-5 business days."

Please practice social distancing: 6 feet = one fully extended trombone

I'm at a place in my life where errands are starting to count as going out.

At this point, my USPS package has a better social life than me.

It's very hard to be both socially distant and Southern.

It's December. The time of year we can wear cozy clothes and stay in. Like the other 11 months of 2020 but more festive.

Yoko Ono sings on city streets to ensure New York residents stay inside.

Who would've thought one day we would be smoking weed at a family gathering, but the illegal part would be the family gathering.

After this plague is over, I don't want to see any more memes claiming you could live in a cabin alone for a full year for $1,000,000. You literally couldn't stay in your house for 5 days to save your grandmother, soooooo…

In other news… The Seven Dwarfs have been advised that as of today, they can only meet in groups of six. One of them isn't Happy.

People are scared of getting fined for congregating in crowds. As if catching a deadly disease and dying a horrible death wasn't enough of a deterrent.

An epidemiologist, an ICU doctor and a scientist walk into a bar… Just kidding, they know better.

My favorite part of social isolation is that I no longer have to think of excuses on why I can't go to social events.

You wanna see social distancing? Loan somebody some money.

Fight Coronavirus! Eat five cloves of garlic every day. It does absolutely nothing, but keeps everyone else at a safe distance.

Enforce social distancing. Eat beans!

They say that for Christmas we can meet up to 8 people without any problems. But I don't know 8 people without problems...

We isolate now so when we gather again, no one is missing.

I don't know who needs to hear this but your choice to give up the last 7 months of your regular life being careful and social distancing could very well be the reason someone else is alive today and it will always have been worth it.

Archery is stabbing with social distancing. Change my mind.

With no one allowed in the water, sharks now have to do curbside pickup.

The good thing about having a social life like mine is that you don't even notice that you are in quarantine.

I'll be honest: not seeing some of you for 3 months has been an absolute delight

Last year I joined a support group for antisocial people. We haven't met yet.

I wonder if the social isolation was long enough for McDonald's to fix the ice cream machine.

Those who have stayed inside, wore masks in public, and socially distanced during this entire pandemic are the same people who are used to doing the whole group project by themselves.

Family Matters including Pets During Lockdown

My 14-year-old wore jeans today that didn't have holes. Maybe the world really is beginning to heal.

It's been a great blessing to be at home with the wife these last few months. We've caught up on everything I've done wrong in the last 20 years.

What did our parents do to kill boredom before the Internet? I asked my 26 brothers and sisters and they didn't know either.

My husband asked if he had any annoying habits and then got all offended during the PowerPoint presentation.

Always remember to be nice to people who have access to your toothbrush.

Remember: When you bury a body, cover it with endangered plants so that it is illegal to dig it up. Follow me for more gardening tips.

Quarantine drinking game: Take a drink every time you hear "Mom!" Just kidding. Don't do that. You will die.

I'm stuck between a rock and someone I'd like to hit with it.

My wife just said that if I don't get off the computer and help her with the dishes, she's going to slam my head into the computer, but I think that she is just jokinqwertyuiop[]sdfghjkl;'Xcvbnm,./3456789

Dads, listen up. Mother's Day is coming on the tail end of a long quarantine home with kids. Go big this year.

Y'all are making your kids soft. When I was 5 I died once and mom made me walk it off…

Question: Due to COVID, I've heard that if you have visitors/relatives drop in unexpectedly over Christmas, the police have the power to come round and force people to go home. Is there are website where you can register/apply for this service and is it free or do you have to pay?

(Brings therapist to family gathering) Me: See? Therapist: Oh. My. God.

Don't tell a mom she looks tired; she already knows that. Tell her she's doing a good job; she might not know that.

I don't understand how God can have 10 Commandments for the whole world, and my wife can have 152 just for our house.

When your kid complains that their toy isn't working anymore, and you have to pretend to be shocked like you didn't take the batteries out.

To everyone who said we hung our door upside down: We did it so our puppies could look out.

Thinking of sleeping on my husband's side of the bed today. Apparently from that side, you don't hear the kids wake up at night.

As we end Week 2 of the lockdown, I've been thinking about Osama bin Laden. He was stuck in his house with three wives for five years. I'm beginning to wonder if he called in those Navy SEALs himself.

Becoming a grandparent is the one time it's acceptable to choose your own nickname and people blow it every time. Why would you be Grampy when you could be DEATH-BLADE!

Department of Health is looking to hire couples married for 7 years or more to educate people on social distancing.

For those weddings cancelled due to COVID-19: God is giving you a second chance to think about it.

If you decide to go through his phone, don't check to see if he's cheating. Go to his bank app and send yourself money. Stop being stupid.

Don't believe what you see in cartoons. No matter how hard you throw a toilet plunger, it won't actually stick to someone's face. Don't ask me how I know this.

When this lockdown is over, if you had to choose between going on a bender with ya mates or taking your mrs. out for a romantic meal, which pub would you meet your mates in?

I just bought my husband a "get better soon" card. He's not sick… I just think he could be better.

90% of parenting is just thinking about when you can lie down again.

I have made many questionable decisions in my life. But right now, having a partner who makes me laugh and shares my love of humor is proving to be one of the best choices I ever made. Hey, kids, marry the funny one. You never know when you'll be quarantined together.

I told my wife how thankful I was to have someone I enjoyed being quarantined with. She said "Must be nice."

Child: Why Not? 2020 Parent: Because of COVID. (The upside of a pandemic.)

There are two things I love more than anything in the world:

1. Being with my kids
2. Not being with my kids

The trick to getting your kids to eat more vegetables is to mix them in with their favorite foods. For example, I like to wedge a few carrot sticks into my daughter's crayon box.

Can you blink a little more quietly, please?

You think you are in charge of your house until your kid gets out of bed and you panic and hide the ice cream you were eating.

This is Bob. He let his wife cut his hair. He called it the Covid Cut. Don't be like Bob.

I don't know why people say having a dog prepares you for having a kid because a dog has never wanted to watch Frozen 47 times in a row.

My husband should be thankful for my multiple personalities. He is quarantined with someone different every day.

Marriage Tip #46: Your wife won't start an argument with you if you're cleaning.

When a woman says "correct me if I'm wrong..." do not under any, I mean any, circumstances do it.

When a man says he'd do anything for a woman, he means he'd stop bullets and slay dragons, not clean the basement and wash dishes.

90% of what I say to my children after 6 p.m. ends with ...or you can go to bed right now.

My family complained that my life revolves around Facebook and affects how we communicate as a family. So I blocked them.

What I say: "Please get dressed." What my son hears: "Please stand naked at the top of the stairs and play Hot Cross Buns on the recorder."

What did you do during the coronavirus, Daddy? Posted a ton of memes to uplift the vibration of the collective consciousness. Freakin' legend.

My son just threatened to not talk to me for the rest of the day. I'm 3% offended and 97% hoping he follows through.

I turned off the tv today and made my kids play board games like it was 1955 and now I know why all of our grandparents were alcoholics.

A fun thing about having teens home during the summer break is that they only require 2 meals a day because they don't wake up until lunch.

My wife is a kindergarten teacher and I think she is using her teaching techniques on me. Because I really enjoy getting a Skittle for putting the toilet seat down.

I'm about to start my own YouTube channel just so my kids will start listening to me.

Do teens' ears actually work or are they just for show?

Having a 2-year-old is like having a blender that you don't have a top for.

That moment when you counted to three but your kid didn't stop and you start wondering if you're actually qualified to be in charge around here.

Before having a kid the most important thing to ask yourself is "Am I ready to watch the exact same cartoon on repeat for the next 4 years?"

(Toddler starts taking his pants off.) Me: Why are you doing that? Toddler: Because I'm sad. Me: You're too sad for pants? Toddler: Yes. Me: Your feelings are valid.

I've heard that women speak 20,000 words a day. I have a daughter who can double that before lunch.

If your kids are bothering you, a fun thing you can say is, "Oh, Good! You're just in time to help me clean the cat litter" and voila! Instant alone time.

Ah, parenting. Yes, that's a crayon in my coffee. And no, I didn't find it until I reached the bottom.

At the end of the quarantine, if you decide you can't stand the people you live with, just remember I am a realtor.

My kids have started removing one letter of bad words, so they can call each other names and not get in trouble. So I've decided to add one digit to the wi-fi password until they can be nice to each other.

My husband just told me he wants a divorce. Actually, his exact words were "I think it would be cool for the whole family to live in an RV and travel the country for a year", but tomato, to-mah-to.

Remember: Having sex on a regular basis helps keep your memory alive. I wish you all a great 2016.

When my wife is mad at me I tighten all the jar lids so she has to talk to me.

Give a kid a bath and they'll be clean all day. Give them a pool and they'll be clean all summer.

Quarantining with kids is like being the only employee in a 24-hour restaurant.

My kids used to have a bedtime… now they just tuck me in and continue doing whatever the heck they want.

I think one reason my dog and I are so close is that we both hate it when I vacuum.

Practical advice: If all toilets in your house are occupied and you are waiting for one to be free, switch off the wi-fi.

Look, I don't like you. You don't like me. But we gotta make this work, for the kids. –me to my swimsuit before taking the kids to the pool

You know you're a parent when 9:15 in the morning feels late in the day.

If you want to save money at Xmas, now's the perfect time to tell the kids that Santa didn't make it through the pandemic.

My husband printed out a picture of a clean sink and put it over the dishes. I think I'm going to murder him.

Since Millennials can't read cursive… We older folks attack at dawn.

Marriage vows should include: "Do you promise to always help him find his stuff that's right in front of him?" because you will be doing that forever.

I'll see your toddler tantrum and raise you a teen that just had their phone taken away.

"Alexa, stop. Alexa, stop! Alexa, STOP!" When you realize Alexa listens to you just about as well as your kids do.

Building Inspector: Well, you say you've kept everything up to code, but I've been speaking with your 4-year-old and he informed me that the floor is actually lava, which—I don't need to tell you—is a pretty serious safety violation.

I just yelled, "1, 2, 3, Mommy is lava!" and my kids ran away, leaving me to drink my coffee in peace. I'm pretty sure I've peaked for the day.

I am convinced that there is a sensor in my butt that alerts my husband and kids in my home of the exact moment I sit down.

Me: (panic) How long has it been since we bathed the kids? Husband: I sprayed them with the garden hose yesterday while washing the car. Me: Oh, thank Goodness. Stay tuned for our parenting book

My wife's superpower is observing when I'm happy and putting a stop to that nonsense.

Husband: When I get mad at you, you never fight back. How do you control your anger? Wife: I clean the toilet. Husband: How does that help? Wife: I use your toothbrush.

When a kid says "Daddy, I want Mommy", that's the kid version of "I'd like to speak to your supervisor."

Husband: "I want you to have this bracelet. It belonged to my grandmother." Wife: "Why does it say 'Do Not Resuscitate'"?

When you have two kids but only 17 cookies left, and can't have them fighting about unfair distribution so you eat all 17 cookies because you're a good parent.

I show affection for my pets by holding them against me and whispering "I love you" as they struggle frantically to escape my arms.

I just read a book on marriage that says treat your wife like you treated her on your first date. So after dinner tonight I'm dropping her off at her parents' house.

Who Was that Masked Man/ Woman?

If you come into our store without a mask, we will have to take your temperature. PS, we only have rectal thermometers. Choose wisely.

Does anyone else rip off their mask when they walk out of a store like they just finished a disappointing surgery on Grey's Anatomy?

Seeing how some people wear their masks, I now understand how contraceptives fail.

Betcha if they discovered that Covid causes permanent impotency, y'all would be wearing those masks like nobody's business.

If there's one thing this year has taught us, it's that Americans are staggeringly selfish. Not just like your meat-and-potatoes "don't want to share" selfish. Total apocalyptic "I will let you die rather than inconvenience myself" selfish.

Flight attendant: In case of emergency, oxygen masks will drop down in front of you. Passenger: You can't force me to wear a mask. I want to speak with the plane manager!

Study Confirms Nose Holes Connect to Lungs. Below-the-nose mask wearers shocked by science.

A friendly reminder: Wearing a mask while alone in a car is only helpful if you stole the car.

What is something you have said in the past 6 months that you would not have in 2019? "Put your mask on; we're going into the bank."

I put on a mask and literally within seconds, I am struggling to breathe… The surgeon who wore a mask for six hours to reconstruct my knee thinks maybe you're lying and also a drama queen.

Mask not what your country can do for you. Mask what you can do for your country.

If you all don't start wearing masks then you are going to have to homeschool your kids this fall. Hope this helps.

Random woman in store: You're supposed to be wearing a mask. Foil: I'm supposed to be wearing underwear, too, yet here we are.

Soooo cities are canceling Halloween? The holiday that is LITERALLY about wearing masks!

If you're wearing a mask inside of your car, I'm gonna go ahead and assume it's to control the urge to lick the windows.

Until you do 30min+ of CPR in a plastic gown, N95, surgical mask, two pairs of gloves and a face shield, you should probably stop complaining about wearing some fabric on your face to the grocery store.

Calm down. Walmart is just asking you to wear a mask. You can still wear your pajamas, and leave your bras and teeth at home.

The ones in the masks are the good guys.

Insisting on your rights without acknowledging your responsibilities isn't freedom, it's adolescence.

PSA: When enjoying a rare piece of double bubble bubble gum, remember to remove your mask. Muscle memory kicks in before the brain does. Just passing this along…

If it's our constitutional right not to wear a mask, what about clothes in general?

My mask broke at the store and I felt like Janet Jackson at the Super Bowl.

The good thing about wearing a mandatory mask is that people who have bad breath will finally realize it.

When the COVID is over, I'm throwing my mask in the air like a graduation cap.

Sure, don't wear a mask. Just remember the brand new interns start in less than 2 weeks… and their last semester of med school was online.

Thou shalt wear a mask in public. –Hygenesis 3:16

Bonus advantage for teachers wearing masks in public: It's harder for students to recognize you!

I wear my mask in public for three reasons:

- Humility: I don't know if I have COVID as it is clear that people can spread the disease before they have symptoms.
- Kindness: I don't know if the person I am near has a child battling cancer, or cares for their elderly mom. While I might be fine, they might not.
- Community: I want my community to thrive, businesses to stay open, employees to stay healthy. Keeping a lid on COVID helps us all.

Please wear a mask. Nothing to do with Coronavirus. Some of y'all just ugly.

Airgasm: Intense pleasure from the air felt on the face when the mask is removed.

You might be a redneck if your face mask is made of coffee filters and duct tape.

If you're one of those people refusing to wear a mask because you're concerned about enough oxygen reaching your brain, don't worry, that ship has sailed.

If I still have to take my shoes off at the airport because of a failed terrorist attack 19 years ago, then you can wear a mask during a pandemic that has killed over 100,000 Americans.

Captain Kirk: "Come on. Either wear the mask or put on the red shirt."

Y'all complain about everything being closed. Now you're complaining about wearing masks inside of places that are open. You know what? Drink the dang disinfectant.

Mr. Rogers would wear a mask and also validate our emotions about why masks feel hard and scary but are still vitally important to wear.

Coming soon: pumpkin spice Covid masks

Look, guys, you can totally have a beard AND properly wear a mask.

Saying that wearing a mask during a pandemic is "living in fear" is like saying that using oven mitts means you're "afraid" of the oven…

The FDA just approved a drug that reduces your chance of getting COVID by 5X. Its trade name is Wearamaskidiot. Side effects include mild inconvenience, possible victim complex, fear of people thinking you are a sheep, being ostracized by your anti-vax plandemic bros, and the power to stop your own asymptomatic transmission as this country stubbornly dives right on into that second wave. Check with your doctor, or really anyone, to see if Wearamaskidiot is right for you.

Imagine if in London during the Blitz there'd been a whole bunch of people who said "I'll turn on my lights if I feel like it."

If you're baffled at all these people who refuse to wear masks, in 1865 they threw a doctor that recommended hand washing in an insane asylum and then beat him to death.

Wear a mask. That is, unless you want to be intubated by a gynecologist intern who did her last semester of med school via Zoom.

After corona, we will have to wear our masks on the back of our heads for two months to get our ears back in place.

Nine months after corona: Who is the father? Don't know; he wore a mask.

I don't know why people are against wearing masks. Masks protect you from coronavirus, yes, but they also protect you from running into people you know in public. Add sunglasses and you are literally in disguise. It's safe to do anything, anywhere, even in your home town. This is my dream.

Masks are the new bra: They aren't comfortable, you only wear them in public, people will notice when you DON'T wear one, and you can now get them in every color pattern and style.

It's a mask. You're not being asked to shove a jar of pickles up your _____.

A guide showing the effectiveness of face masks, if none, one, or two people wear masks. Zero Risk if both wear masks, and one is playing an accordion 1.5 meters away from the other guy.

Romance novels written during COVID-19 will be like: "and then she slowly slipped her mask down, revealing her warm red lips, and her blushed faced, and as their eyes met, he gently removed her gloves."

Warning: Bridge Washed Out. Unless you feel that this is an attempt to deprive you of your liberty, then keep driving.

Treat your mask like underwear.

- Do not touch or adjust (especially in public)
- Do not borrow or lend
- Make sure it fits tight but comfortably
- Make sure it's clean (daily or as needed)
- Wear the right side out
- If there's holes in it, throw it away
- If it's stained, throw it away
- If it's damp, change it

The Reopening

Let's have a moment of silence for all those teachers setting an alarm for tomorrow.

I love how we as a country watched adults fail miserably at social distancing but are convinced kindergarteners will figure it out.

If a supervisor at work gets the Covid do the people who kiss that ass need to be tested? Asking for a friend.

If you believe all this will end and we will get back to normal once we reopen everything… Raise Your Hand. Now slap yourself with it.

As we say here in Georgia: Happy Re-Infection Day!

The end of stay-at-home orders doesn't mean the pandemic is over. It means they currently have room for you in the ICU.

Having idiots insist we open everything up will have one good effect. Finally, Stupidity will die out.

I don't care about shopping or restaurants... when do Grandparents open back up?

The government in Egypt has instructed the city's taxi drivers to drive around Cairo sounding their car horns. It's hoped that a return to familiar city sounds will help restore calm following the pandemic. Operation Toot And Calm 'Em will last for a week.

Whoever decided a liquor store is more essential than a hair salon is obviously a bald-headed alcoholic.

Due to COVID-19, we are asking rioters to work from home and destroy their own property.

Having some states lock down and some states not lock down is like having a peeing section in a swimming pool.

Do you know how lucky we are that this virus won't spread at grocery stores, big retailers and hardware stores? It's crazy how it only spreads at small businesses.

I just... keep seeing people on social media eating at restaurants, traveling, doing whatever and I'm sitting in my apartment like I've hallucinated a pandemic.

Vying for Vaccines

First photo of the Russian vaccine: Smirnoff

So let me get this straight: There's no cure for a virus that can be KILLED by sanitizer and hand soap?

So… you've been eating hot dogs and McChickens all your life, but don't want the vaccine, because "you don't know what's in it"?

I have faith in Pfizer and its Covid vaccine because it also makes Viagra. If Pfizer can raise the dead it can save the living.

Guys, just to let you know I had the Russian Covid19 vaccination yesterday and can tell you there are absolutely no negative side effects whatsoeveя, and that I feelshкι χoposhό я чувствую себя немного странно и я думаю, что вытащил ослиные уши.

Here's something we can all agree on: the vaccine should be tested on politicians first. If they survive, the vaccine is safe. If they don't, the country is safe.

Apparently, walking around WalMart with an Alka-Seltzer in my mouth yelling "the vaccine isn't working" isn't funny…

I've got 99 problems, but tetanus, diphtheria, pertussis, measles, mumps, rubella rotavirus, influenza, varicella, HIB, hepatitis A & B, pneumococcus, and polio ain't one.

Everyone who received the first smallpox vaccine in 1798 has died. Makes you think…

North Carolina's vaccine will be vinegar based, while South Carolina's will be mustard based.

The vaccine rollout order will be first to those keyworkers for whom it is most vital they can continue to work, and so will therefore be as follows

1. First sopranos
2. Second basses
3. Second altos
4. Second sopranos
5. First basses
6. First altos
7. Organist
8. Conductor
9. Tenors

If you think there are "microchips" in vaccines – chill – you're probably not worth tracking.

Random Words of Wisdom

Not to alarm anyone… but Mad Max took place in 2021

Only when normal things are not normal anymore, do we realize how special normal things are.

It's never explicitly stated how the Brady Bunch had access to Zoom in the 1970s.

Coronacoaster. Noun: The ups and downs of a pandemic. One day you're loving your bubble, doing work outs, baking banana bread and going for long walks and the next you're crying, drinking gin for breakfast and missing people you don't even like.

According to Greek mythology, Chiron was half horse, half human doctor. This made him the Centaur for Disease Control.

The clocks go forward next weekend. Not sure how far forward but I think 4 months should do.

Actually, it's only quarantine if it comes from the Quarantine region of France; otherwise, it's just sparkling isolation.

Due to recent events, the light at the end of the tunnel has been switched off.

Check up on your conspiracy theory friends. They haven't had a day off in weeks.

They asked the Amish why Covid-19 did not affect them. They said, "we don't have TV."

You can't fix stupid, but you can watch it in action on Facebook every day.

For whenever two or three gather in my name, there am I with them. -Covid 1:9

There's a "spike" in Corona cases because there's a spike in testing. If we gave more IQ tests there'd be a spike in morons, too.

Dance like nobody is watching. Text and email like it will be read in court some day.

And you may ask yourself: Did I brush my teeth today? And you may ask yourself: Did I take a shower? David Byrne under quarantine

I was told there would be a handbasket.

Best quotation for 2020: This is not the year to get everything you want. This is the year to appreciate everything you have.

Social media has made too many of you comfortable with disrespecting people and not getting punched in the mouth for it.

My conspiracy theory is that time travel IS real and someone keeps trying to fix 2020 by changing something but every time they do, they unwittingly make it worse.

Am I an uneducated imbecile prone to conspiracy theory? No, it's the doctors who are wrong.

Just wait until conspiracy theorists discover that they're part of a conspiracy to use conspiracy theorists to spread disinformation via conspiracy theories.

Breaking news alert: Tonight at 10 p.m., a medical satellite will fly over the United States to take everyone's temperature. Please stand naked in your driveway with your ID up in the air. Your test results will be mailed to you in 14 days.

Back in my day we just had one idiot per village. These days we've got whole cities full of 'em!

This is the longest something made in China has ever lasted.

Oh, the Places You'll Stay, by Dr. Fauci. You'll stay on the couch! You'll stay in your room! You'll stay in a chair for a meeting on Zoom! You'll stay in the bathroom—a brief getaway! There are so many places at home you will stay.

Did you know that 97% of the world is stupid? Luckily, I'm in the other 5%.

Have you ever noticed that all the instruments searching for intelligent life are pointed away from Earth?

A Special 2020 Side Show: The Murder Hornets

Shout out to the murder hornets for having the decency to be like "we'll come back when it's more convenient for you."

Everyone is freaking out about murder hornets and Texans are wondering how it'll taste stuffed in a jalapeno and wrapped in bacon.

Hmm. Murder hornets. We've reached the stage in the Hunger Games when they've released the Tracker Jackers.

So these murder hornets, do you send them a list of names or what? How does this work?

1,000 murder hornets found dead in Georgia. They met our mosquitos who live on Meth Blood.

Gonna get this out of the way now: drinking bug spray will not protect you from the murder hornets.

This just in: Murder hornets declare US too unsafe to infest. More at 10.

Yes, hi. I ordered rock hard abs and less stress for 2020 but instead got a pandemic and murder hornets. Can I speak to a manager?

The writers' room for 2020 is terrible! You don't put a small earthquake in the middle of a race revolution AND a pandemic story line. Also you don't just introduce murder hornets in like the 3rd episode and then do NOTHING with them! Take a workshop, 2020!

How much toilet paper am I supposed to buy for this murder hornet scare?

Quick question: Are we buying up all the Raid now or throwing toilet paper at the hornets?

Haikus

Unmasked by Sue Jones

Eyes above the mask—
sad, scared, kind, loving, joyful
Windows to the soul

Fear by Sue Jones

Air engulfing masks,
deadly particles assault,
Unseen danger lurks

Home Alone by Sue Jones

Welcome mat removed
visitors not entering
Loneliness abides

Exercise Time by Ruth Van Alstine

Oh, treadmill of mine
sweet love/hate relationship
daily power play

☼

Best Laid Plans by Ruth Van Alstine

reunion pursued
masked airline travel braved
foiled by quarantine

☼

Dazed by Ruth Van Alstine

Months of solitude
Zoomed out, fried on Netflix shows
Coronal doldrums

☼

Strung Out by Ruth Van Alstine

hair-do disaster
toilet paper stockpile low
insanity looms

Limericks

Web Mistress by Sue Jones

A lovely fair Florida lass
Oft admired herself in the glass
Now she scrubs and she mends
Counts spiders as friends,
And for Cinderella could pass.

Face Covering by Carol Pierskalla

There once were some folks from Racine
Who thought face covering obscene!
So they went without masks,
Drank from the same flasks,
And came down with Covid-19

Meanwhile, at the Zoo by Pat Krause

The gates are all locked at the zoo
We animals are in quarantine too

There's no one to see us
so maybe they'll free us
If we promise to wear face masks like you!

Ovid Vs. Covid by Ed Mickolus

The famous philosopher Ovid
Wanted to avoid getting Covid
Funny you should ask
Yes, he wore a mask
But he died when he couldn't rhyme Covid

And a Whole Bunch of Limericks from Greg Barry:

We should heed to the guy we call Fauci.
The vaccine makes the weak ones say "Ouchy."
We'll get out of this soon.
Let the economy boon.
Don't ask Trump 'cuz he always seems grouchy.

– ☺ –

We must deal with this bug named Corona.
To say hoax is completely bologna.
While the virus still looms.
Let's just stay in our rooms.
And keep playing the song "My Sharona."

– ☺ –

To begin it was thought as endemic.
Soon after it became a pandemic.
It couldn't be tamed.
Covid it was named.
In bodies it's quickly systemic.

There once was a virus named Covid.
It infected a guy known as Joe-Kid.
They discovered a cure.
Some dude said it was pure.
No one thought it would work except Joe did.

– ☺ –

There once was a serious virus.
A cure or vaccine was desirous.
We needed good news.
To get over the blues.
A strong leader emerged to inspire us.

– ☺ –

Far too many the virus contracted.
But Congress kept getting distracted.
There's a group called Warp Speed.
A shut down was decreed.
But the process was still quite protracted.

– ☺ –

Pfizer's vaccine must be kept in a freezer.
Tho' its results are a genuine pleaser.
But it may not arrive.
Cuz' I'm below sixty-five.
I can't get it till I'm an old geezer.

– ☺ –

The months crawl by slowly as ever.

When it ends many say it may never.
Let's all get through it whole.
So we can get on a roll.
When we're free we can strive to endeavor.

– ☺ –

If this scourge was begun by a sadist.
While this rhyme may not be the greatest.
Wet Markets be damned.
Our folks have been slammed.
For plagues, this is simply the latest.

– ☺ –

There once was a young man named Harry.
People came to him because things were scary.
He said don't be afraid.
I will come to your aid.
This disease quite soon we will bury.

The Importance of Being Meme

Was 2020 a good year? For who? The human race, no. People that make memes, yes.

Don't think of yourself as a meme thief. Think of yourself as a digital media redistribution agent.

Your meme dealer has played an important part in helping you get through 2020.

I don't mean to brag, but my posts are enjoyed by well over 2 people worldwide.

When people ask me what my spiritual gift is: Memes

The amount of jokes about coronavirus has reached worrying numbers. Scientists claim we are in the middle of a pun-demic.

@coronavirus Honestly, I did it for the memes.

And if you're looking for a scholarly reason why it's ok for you to like memes, try this:

> *"COVID Memes: Why We're Using Laughter To Get Us Through a Pandemic"*
> By Karine Bengualid
> https://copyhackers.com/2020/06/covid-memes/

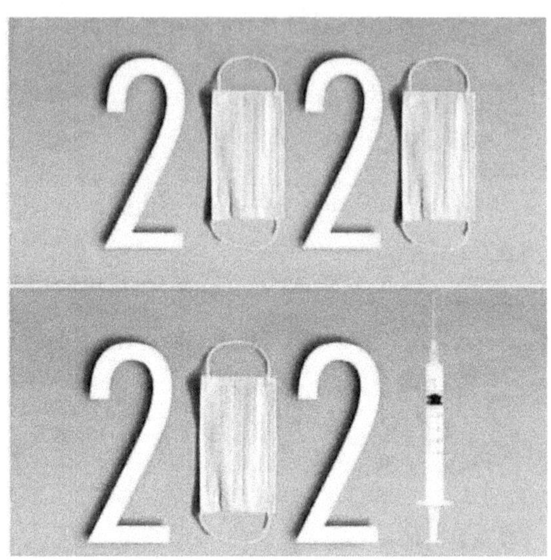

The official DIY Christmas ornament for 2020 😂

www.ingramcontent.com/pod-product-compliance
Lightning Source LLC
Chambersburg PA
CBHW061745050726
47598CB00002B/595

9781949173109